The Butterfly ChaSu

Susan Glenn Lampe

Illustrations by Karen Murley

The Butterfly ChaSu
Copyright © 1995 Susan Glenn Lampe
Published by WinePress Publishing
PO Box 1406, Mukilteo, WA 98275

Printed in Canada.

ISBN 1-883893-21-6

About The Butterfly ChaSu

I've read that wing flaps of a butterfly can shape the world and that the loss of one butterfly reverberates throughout the universe.

The story, The Butterfly ChaSu settled on me in 1983, and I typed the original words on the last days of one of the best jobs I ever held, during the darkest years of my life.

For twelve years, I've watched this story undergo metamorphosis, buffeted by rejection and change. Perhaps we clung to each other, ChaSu and I, as we both emerged from our cocoons.

Something nudged me last spring to consider self-publication. Weeks later, I met Athena Dean from WinePress Publishing and within months, ChaSu was freed to fly.

Many visualize ChaSu as a children's story though this was never my intention. Certainly, some of the characters are children and the story borders on fact —there are real lepidopterists, real butterfly farms, and real butterflies that migrate (though most live weeks not years) and real children in classrooms who listen to butterfly stories and study this magnificent insect. For me, ChaSu's lessons echo more deeply into shades of letting go of people, places and things, into an awareness of ecology's fragile balance between man and things of the wild—plant, mammal, insect, fish, including the shadows of vibrant blue butterflies who fly no more.

ChaSu's most valuable lesson remained hidden from me many years. Why must Chadworth release the butterfly? Why couldn't she free herself? I questioned this as I struggled to stand upright as a woman. All efforts to reshape the story's end failed until I understood that ChaSu's freedom from Chadworth's hands symbolizes compatibility of men and women with neither being in control. In my experience, men and women function best as equals, when they appreciate each other's gifts and learn from one another. If ChaSu freed herself, she'd have no need of Chadworth but she did need him to raise and shape her, to teach and guide her.

I thank the sender of this story for these twelve years with ChaSu, and I choose to believe that sender is God. ChaSu and I journeyed many roads together and she comforted me. Through this book, I send her forth in hopes that her messages may be heard and treasured by others.
God Bless,

Susan Lampe

Dedication

This book is dedicated to those who've
taught me most about letting go—
my mother and father,
Chuck, Mindy, Thom,
Becca and Rich.

"When I was your age, I lived on a butterfly farm."   I'd attracted the third graders' attention so I lowered my voice. They ceased wriggling, tucked their legs beneath their bodies or stuck them straight out. They stopped whispering and poking and shifted their eyes to mine. Spring sun kaleidoscoped about us as we huddled on the schoolroom floor.

"Close your eyes," I told them. "Picture dusky-blue mists over snow-capped mountains. Purple, blue, and yellow wildflowers explode from rocky crevices in summer. Aspen trees color fields golden in fall, and the fierce white snows of winter blind and halt the activity of all men and animals.

"The butterflies add magic. They arrive every spring by thousands in a multitude of wings. Their presence stirs barely a murmur in the brief moments of twilight given to the mountains.

"My mother, Suzanne, discovered them first."

The children's eyes and mouths opened as I wrapped them into my tale. "Do you think this sounds like a magic place?" Heads nodded one way or another; some turned, sought their teacher.

"My grandparents lived for years on this magical mountain estate. When they died, Father moved our family there, but I felt isolated when winter winds roared and buried our brick home in snow and kept me from my friends. I escaped down the mountain only for school.

My parents also seemed lonely until the wild butterflies landed on our ridge that first spring. Father got the idea to restore a greenhouse to breed butterflies. My parents became lepidopterists, specialists in the study of moths and butter-flies.

They talked about one special female butterfly from Asia with rare colors of blue and purple. They discussed her at supper as the three of us ate at our massive mahogany table. Mother and I sat across from each other, separated by Father at the head and a candelabra holding six candles.

"Suzanne!" Father's fist pounded the table. "I must have that butterfly!" Dark hair curled against his neck and cheeks; he rose to pace back and forth.

"Mother!" I mouthed the word silently. I searched for her gentle smile. My stomach ached when Father spoke so loudly.

"Chadworth," her quiet voice soothed. "Why not buy this butterfly? I've never seen a purple-blue butterfly, have you Colleen?" She smiled at me, a smile of honey sweetness, of healing love and patience, her kitten gray eyes flecked by gold.

*   *   *

Our second spring on the ridge, when the wet ground firmed and the air became tinged with warm wind, Mother and I scanned the skies for the wild butterflies.

One night she awakened me. We crept outside into the darkness and hid beside a rotting, fallen log near the ridge. In the dim haze of early morning light, we saw shadows of thousands of butterflies covered the ground. They quietly opened and shut their black and gold wings, lifted thin legs in a myriad of small miracles displayed before us. In the sun's first rays, as the butterflies spread wings to the warmth, they began to ascend on wind currents. I grabbed Mother's arm to show her that some looked translucent, barely blue in the light. She nodded. "Those are very rare," she whispered.

Mother and I never watched the butterflies together again. A few days later, she rode off on her horse and never returned. A search party figured the horse slipped in the mud and fell from the mountain. No trace of my mother or her horse was ever found. Some thought she tried to follow the butterflies. I knew only that I would never see my mother again.

I waited for the children to absorb this before I continued. "How Father changed! Gruff and frightening before, he now seemed gigantic. He boomed out daily commands. I could never please him. He studied his butterflies, trapped and dissected some, created tiny obstacle courses for others to climb in, out, around, or through. He wrote articles for magazines and became well-known for butterfly research.

"It doesn't hurt them," he'd say, and chop off their wings. I didn't believe him. In the fall, he bought and fetched home a valuable Far Eastern butterfly. He called her ChaSu. He combined the first letters of his name with my mother's (CHA for Chadworth and SU for Suzanne). I loved to watch ChaSu's fragile, transparent wings in different rays of light. Her colors reminded me of amethyst.

I think Father came as close to loving ChaSu as he'd loved anyone, even Mother. She rode on his shoulder when they strolled our estate. He confided in her as he'd never confided in me.

After school, I'd slip through the screen door of the greenhouse, creep soundlessly across the flagstone floors to rock in Father's old oak chair and be with ChaSu while I worked on homework.

One spring evening I dozed, legs curled beneath a patch quilt. I dreamed of Mother. I woke to dawn's light and sensed the butterflies had landed on the ridge. I raced for the door and ChaSu flew to my shoulder. Together we glimpsed a flutter of wings—butterflies rising!

What does a captured butterfly know of freedom? Within days, ChaSu began to soar up and away from Father's shoulder during their strolls. She'd disappear into the sky before she returned.

Frightened of losing her, Father cried, "ChaSu! What does this mean?" If she left, his voice echoed around the ridge, "Find ChaSu! Find ChaSu!"

"She'll come back, Father," I'd assure him. One day, when she'd returned after an exceptionally long escapade, Father popped a jar over her, then screwed the lid on. After that he kept her encased in a cage within the greenhouse.

"ChaSu," I whispered. I nearly cried to see her drooping wings and faded colors.

That winter, ChaSu hid when Father neared her cage. He no longer let her leave the greenhouse. She'd grown too old to be bred but her early offspring sported her purple and blue colors like tiny photograph copies of their mother. As the snow melted, I'd find her at the corner, on the hard-packed dirt greenhouse floor methodically scraping with her small black legs, as if trying to dig out.

While I watched her doing this one spring evening, I sensed the butterflies return; their flocking created a small cloud between me and the sun. ChaSu flew instantly to the screen door.

All night I sat in my upstairs window, faced the ridge and wondered what to do. By morning, I knew.

I asked the children, "What do you think I should have done? What would you have done?"

"Free her! Free her!"

*   *   *

I crept from my room at the earliest sign of light. I skirted squeaky places in the hall and stairway floorboards, cursed the rubber stair runners that slowed me. I reached the massive oak and glass doorway that led outside, tugged it open and stepped into a golden morning. Butterflies filled the sky! I turned toward the greenhouse, then stopped to see Father's silhouette etched against the doorway. Time slowed.

I watched him open the door. ChaSu perched on his shoulder. They moved in tandem. Father twitched his shoulder slightly and the butterfly rose. She floated into the cerulean morning sky. Below, Father and I must have seemed specks as she gained altitude and joined the multitude while they lifted into the first full rays of sun.

THE END

About the Author

Susan Glenn Lampe wrote <u>The Butterfly ChaSu</u> in 1983, while she lived in St. Louis, Missouri, and worked for a hospital there as public relations director. She received a bachelor of journalism degree in 1967, from the University of Missouri, Columbia. While living in Rochester, New York, she returned to school at State University of New York (SUNY) Brockport, and received a master's degree in creative writing in 1993. Today, she writes and teaches in Edmonds, Washington.

About the Illustrator

Karen Murley is an illustrator and graphic designer who operates Full Circle Design in Cerro Gordo, Illinois. Karen has a BFA in painting from Denison University in Granville, Ohio, and did post-graduate work at the University of Miami. She holds an Art Specialist certificate and taught art to young children and teens. Until 1989, she was designer/art director in several design and advertising studios in the Washington, D.C. area.

Susan Glenn Lampe and Karen Murley first met while in elementary school in Decatur, Illinois in the 1950's.

To order additional copies of **The Butterfly ChaSu**
Send $6.95* (price includes shipping and handling) to:

Susan Glenn Lampe
PO Box 802
Edmonds, WA 98020

*Bookstore discounts available
by calling (206) 672-2037.